The Journey of Faith & Finance

14 Days of Transformational Prayers

ISBN: 979-8-9994972-0-8

Self-Published by Shavonna Perkins

www.shavonnaperkins.com

SHAVONNA PERKINS

The Journey of Faith & Finance

14 Days of Transformational Prayers

DEDICATION

This book is for anyone who's ever quietly wondered, "When will I get "there?" If you've prayed through uncertainty, carried silent burdens, or questioned if God hears your needs, this is for you. I hope that as you reflect, you'll find peace in His presence, clarity for your next step, and a renewed trust that He is your provider both in the waiting and in the breakthrough.

TABLE OF CONTENTS

INTRODUCTION

Trust me, I get it: life can happen fast and throw curveballs, leaving you with nothing to say but **HELP**. Life, especially your financial life, can at times be like one intense game of tug-of-war. Some days, you are the strong one holding your own; others, you're being pulled harder than you ever knew possible. However, deep down inside, you know there is more for you, and the victory is already yours. But you can't help but wonder how that "more" is supposed to unfold and how victory will reveal itself. Well, that's the part that can leave you feeling stuck.

As if that wasn't enough, let's throw in a lack of confidence, clarity, and commitment into the mix. Talk about a ball of confusion! But let me tell you something: you are not alone or misunderstood. You serve a God who hears every frustrated sigh, understands the unspoken worries buried in your heart, and translates them into a language of love and care. He's waiting, eager to meet you right where you are, even in the middle of chaos.

This is me, Shavonna, sitting down with you, sharing what I've learned as I walk this faith journey. I promise I won't pretend I've got it all together. Honestly, I'm struggling with my fair share. If you ask me, mindset and identity issues took too long, making me feel smaller than the dreams God had put in my heart; dreams that took money, BIG money. I consulted with him several times, asking if He had the right person. While the money to fund these dreams seemed scarce, it wasn't always about not having enough; sometimes, it was feeling unworthy to receive God's blessings and being caught up in doubt. But prayer is changing that. I really can't explain it another way. Over the next fourteen days, you will walk through prayers, scripture, and thoughtful questions designed to move you from financial fear and uncertainty into confidence, clarity, and peace.

I'll tell you a secret: things started changing when I stopped trying to fix everything on my own and started talking with God. While the independent woman in me still attempts to fix things in my strength and becomes frustrated when it doesn't work, I realized something important: many of us are stuck, not because the resources aren't available, but simply because we haven't sought God for the how and location of the resources. The more I prayed, the more I realized that God wasn't some distant, disinterested being. On the contrary, He was right there, desiring to lead me through every financial challenge, mental block, and self-imposed limitation. I've lived through moments where God's provision left me speechless, where doors opened that I never even knew existed, and where I finally began to understand what financial freedom really meant.

You see, these prayers aren't just words I threw together in a devotional. They come from the chapters of my story: revelation, surrender, and breakthrough. You will see that I quickly realized that my finances were just a byproduct of everything else but not the root and foundation of my struggles. Once I got to the root, I saw a change. Everything you're about to experience will have its way back into your **prayer life**. These prayers aren't a dialogue between me and you; they are meant for you and God alone. Think of me as just a friend who's had some disappointments, discovered the power of connecting with God through prayer, and now wants to hand you what I found while still discovering who and where God is taking me. Learn to listen carefully, trust deeply, and let Him guide your heart, mind, and financial decisions.

I think about the prophet Habakkuk, standing before God in a time of chaos, not fearing to ask, "Why?" and "When?"—questions I know I have asked more than a few times. And then came this word from God: simple, yet oh-so powerful, to him: "Write the vision and make it plain." Even when things seem to be standing still, God is never off the clock, and He never forgets His people. That is a promise on which we can stand, even if the ground is shaky.

What stands out to me about Habakkuk is that he didn't just speak *to* God; he paused long enough to hear *from* Him. He created space for a true dialogue. He questioned. He waited. He listened. He positioned himself intentionally, taking time to reflect rather than react, and to sit still long enough to receive God's instruction. And God answered back, even when the response wasn't what Habakkuk expected or wanted to hear. His conversation with God was an attempt to make sense of what he was witnessing in real time—violence, injustice, and uncertainty that didn't align with his beliefs about God's character. Even his name, derived from the Hebrew verb *ḥavak*, reflects a kind of clinging or wrestling. An image of someone holding tightly to God while struggling to understand divine justice. Habakkuk teaches us that faith doesn't mean silence; it means staying connected long enough to be shaped, corrected, and directed by what God reveals.

Today's world might look a lot like Habakkuk's: confusing, uncertain, and downright frustrating. But just like then, God hasn't stopped being faithful. I want you to see over the next few days that you don't have to figure it all out alone. You may find yourself wrestling with God over what you see happening around you, what feels unfair, delayed, or unclear. Especially as it relates to your finances. Through the meditation of these scriptures, the questions you're given, and the prayers you're praying, create space to reflect and listen for God's instructions—how He wants you to move, steward, pause, or prepare. Stay resilient. Stay present. Don't quit the conversation. See yourself through this season, trusting that what God is doing in you and through you is purposeful, even when it's still unfolding.

Prayer changed how I view finances, my future, my potential, and God. It transformed my mindset from "not enough" to "more than enough," breaking off those limiting beliefs and patterns that tell you that you'll always struggle or "there" is just a dream. I've seen it happen.

I've lived it. And I know it can happen for you, too. I now have no other option but to dream and believe BIG.

As you go through this devotional, I pray that you will come to realize that prayer is more than an item on your spiritual "to-do" list. But a lifeline of communication to the One who sees your needs, knows your fears, and cares about your future more than you could imagine. Learn to align your heart with God's heart and trust Him even when all around you says panic. It is all about realizing that the real wealth God has for you is not in your bank account; it is how you think, believe, and step out in faith; it is about freedom. And while faith is the foundation, faith alone is not a financial plan. That is why this devotional is titled Faith + Finance. The two do not magically collide and make everything better. Instead, faith builds your foundation, but stewardship and wise management of your finances determine whether you will only survive on "just enough" or finally step into the fullness of life God has for you.

So, let's settle in. You might feel challenged, maybe even a little uneasy at times, as God reveals areas of growth. But trust me, this journey is worth it. We will lean into prayer together, knowing that God is listening and ready to respond. This isn't a journey about perfection; it's about connection. I am excited to see what God will do as you pray for the financial freedom He wants. You'll come out on the other side with a stronger faith, a clearer vision, and a deeper understanding that God cares about your finances, but he cares about YOU.

Find a quiet place, take a moment to center yourself, grab a journal if you need more room for writing and reflection, turn on your favorite worship music or this specially curated Apple playlist, "The Journey of Faith & Finance: 14 Days of Transformational Prayers," and create an atmosphere that invites real change. As you read, let the melodies support the words you read. The prayers, scriptures, and songs together will help usher you into a posture of faith, thankfulness, and expectation, welcoming the presence of God into your mind, heart, and even your financial journey.

My Prayer for You, the Reader:

Heavenly Father, I lift to you every reader holding this devotional in their hands. I ask that you protect their mind, heart, and spirit as they move through the next fourteen days. Cover them with your peace. Grant them consistency in their efforts, strengthen their faith in your promises, and prepare their hearts to receive all you have in store for them. You see exactly where they stand and that they are willing to grow and trust in you.

Lord, I pray these words will not be mere ink on a page, but with every sentence, something will be stirred deep in their soul, stirring real change. May they never falter in knowing that you are at work, no matter the challenges they face. You are the God of more than enough, and I trust that you will do more than they could ever imagine, providing abundant blessings far beyond their hopes and dreams.

Father, you see every heart; you know every story. Whether they are feeling joyful or carrying a heavy burden, uncertain about their next steps, or in dire need of a miracle, Lord, you understand their circumstances completely. I pray that you meet them where they are, showing up in their situations with compassion, guidance, and hope.

Remind them that they do not have to be perfect to approach you. For those whose heads are hanging low because of discouragement, those souls feeling battered by life's storms, and those holding on with nothing, but a whisper of prayer left, I pray that you restore their strength. Give them the courage to face another day, the peace that surpasses all understanding, and the confidence that you are with them in every moment.

I ask that testimonies arise from this journey—stories of renewed vision, unexpected provision, and unshakable confidence in you. Remind each reader that they are your child and joint heirs with your Son. Please give them the clarity to pursue new opportunities, the courage to continue through difficulties, and the confidence to commit and remain steadfast when the path seems steep.

No matter how intimidating the road ahead may be, help them to keep their eyes fixed on you. May their trust in your goodness and sovereignty never fail. I thank you, God, for what you will accomplish in their lives through this time of dedicated reflection and prayer. In Jesus' name, Amen.

FAITH + FINANCE

Now, before we get into Day 1, let me take a minute to tell you about two incredible people from the Bible who, through studying, have shaped my perspective on faith, life, and yes finances. Let me introduce you to my guy David and my girl Ruth. They are like spiritual mentors who showed me what it looks like to trust God through twists, turns, and all life's unexpected detours.

First up: David. You've probably heard a thing or two about him taking down Goliath. But trust me, there's so much more to his story. David was the kind of man who had a promise from God yet had to live a whole bunch of "regular life" before ever stepping into that promise fully and tended sheep long before wearing a crown. David stayed faithful in the little tasks even when people overlooked him because he knew God was watching. When the world around him screamed that he was too small, too young, too outnumbered, David didn't flinch. He saw everything through the eyes of faith and believed in God's timing so much that he refused to push his agenda. David patiently waited, trusting that God was in control.

And get this: David's confidence didn't come from his résumé; it came from knowing that God was the real hero of his story. He gave

God the credit for every breakthrough, every season of favor, and every new responsibility he was entrusted with. He understood that his destiny wasn't about maximizing his ego. It was about serving something bigger than himself. When David stepped up to face a giant or lead a nation, he went in with a heart, convinced that if God said it, He'd make it happen. That's the kind of faith I want to bring into my finances. A faith that doesn't crumble when the numbers look off, waits on God's promotion instead of forcing things, and trusts God's ability to do the impossible.

Now, onto Ruth, my girl who shows us what stepping out in faith really looks like. Ruth left behind what was comfortable and familiar to follow her mother-in-law, Naomi, to a land she didn't know. She had every reason to turn back, to say, "This is too much," but she pressed forward, believing that God could write a beautiful story out of her obedience. Ruth's life teaches us that we need God to help us reach a point where His word and our life are saying the same thing, where we're not just talking about trust but living it. I had to ask God to take control and move me out of that "hidden" stage where I was focused on my insecurities and into a place where His presence shines through me, and fundamental transformation happens. Ruth's humility, willingness to embrace change, and faith to step into the unknown shows us that when we let God lead, He redefines what's possible.

So why talk about these two before we even start Day 1? Because David and Ruth show us that trusting God is a whole-life endeavor; it touches everything, including our finances. Like Solomon, another biblical giant I love studying and noted as the wealthiest man ever to live, they remind us that when we pray for wisdom and God to guide us, we're not just mumbling words. We're setting our foundation with Him, inviting God to align our hearts with His, to strengthen our faith muscles, and to prepare us by giving us the wisdom for handling the blessings we can't imagine. The Bible says that when Solomon didn't ask for wealth or riches but wisdom, it pleased God. In that moment, then He added wealth, honor, and long life (1 Kings 3:10-15). We're learning to see through the eyes of faith as David did, ask for wisdom like Solomon, and be open to change and growth, like Ruth was. It's about believing God's promises so deeply that even when nothing looks right, we stand firm in obedience, knowing He can still move mountains.

Now that you have had the chance to recall the stories of these faithful trailblazers, let's continue writing our stories. Next is Day 1, and I can't wait to see how God uses these prayers to shape your perspective, shift your mindset, and show you what's possible when your finances are surrendered to Him.

DAY 1
I AM THANKFUL

"Oh give thanks to the LORD, for He is good; for His steadfast love endures forever!" ~ 1 Chronicles 16:34

As I stood outside our home, watching our two kids play with our 7-month-old puppy, tears streamed down my face, and I began to thank God. Not solely for the material possessions but for being in my right mind, having a healthy family, and having a real relationship with Him. One not inherited from my parents or tied to just going to church but something personal and genuine. The kind where His presence unintentionally overtakes you as you sit in the middle of traffic. But at that moment, standing outside our home, it struck me that what I was living today once felt like a far-off dream. It was one of those visions that sounded good in theory, but I had no clue how or if it would become a reality. It was the kind of life, as a child, that I'd only seen on TV. The biggest revelation is that it was indeed an answered prayer.

A few weeks before writing this devotional, I stumbled upon my old high school Senior Memories book from 2005. I know we just started, but let's take a pause. A pause for all of those like me, sitting in the fact that it's been 20 years since our high school graduation. But let's not dwell on that too long; I found the "Dreams & Goals" page, which said, "Set your sights for the future and 'predict' where you'll be ten years from now." Looking back, I know I wasn't making predictions; just dreaming, hoping, and believing. I had written:

- Education: NC State University
- Career: Accountant
- Family: Married with 2 Kids
- Home: In NC, with a house built from the ground up (clearly, I meant a custom home, being that most homes are built from the ground!).

Little did I know all this and more would come together within 10 years, with our second child being born only a few years later. Sure, I'm not an accountant (I didn't ask God about that!), but I graduated from NC State University with an Accounting degree. I'm still helping people navigate their finances, I'm happily married with two kids, and we're living in our second property; a home where we picked the layout, the design, the colors, and all the finishing touches. Oh, and did I mention I'm driving the dream car I picked out in high school?

Don't get me wrong: the journey here, and even life now, isn't all roses. I am still required to seek God daily for guidance. If I'm honest, the seeking must increase with each new level. But I'm thankful because appreciation matters. Too often, we complain about what we don't have and forget to thank God for the prayers He's already answered. When we overlook gratitude, it's like pouring water on fire. We quench the warmth, glow, and beauty of what God does in our lives.

The first step in aligning our faith and finances is to recognize that God is the ultimate source of all we have, thus responding with sincere thanks. Honestly, who knows where I'd be if I got what I deserved for the bitterness I once held (cue the dramatic eye roll)? But prayer led me to thankfulness, and in that space, God reminded me that I have access; the same access Christ and even Abraham had (Romans 5:2; Genesis 12:1-3). Knowing this helps break every limit I thought existed. My gratitude takes root in that truth, and my sense of expectancy grows because I genuinely believe God is willing and able to move on my behalf.

A heart full of gratitude softens the ground for real transformation. An attitude of expectancy proves our faith is alive and ready to see more of God's goodness. Today, I choose thankfulness, far beyond my finances. Simply for life, health, strength, and most importantly, a loving and forgiving Father who saw me in my mess yet still gave His Son so I could be restored, redeemed, and made right with Him. I am ultimately grateful for the greatest gift of all: a relationship with God through Jesus Christ, who loves me through all of life's happenings. That kind of love is an action that can never be repaid, reduced, or replaced. And because of that, I have no doubt and am fully expecting that the days ahead will be nothing short of life changing.

Prayer

Heavenly Father,

I come before you with a heart full of gratitude, humility, and faith. Thank you for being Alpha and Omega, the beginning and the end. Lord, I acknowledge you as my ultimate source, provider, and sustainer. Thank you, Lord, for the dreams you've placed within me, for I know you are ready to bring them to life. Every good and perfect gift comes from you, and for that, I give you praise. Thank you for all that you are doing, for the ways you have provided in the past, and for the blessings you are preparing for my future.

Today, as I start this fourteen-day journey with a spirit of expectancy, I know you are a God who keeps His promises, and your word does not return void. Lord, I believe you have plans for my good, to give me hope and a future. As I seek you throughout this journey, I thank you for revealing wisdom, understanding, and strategies for my finances that align with your will.

God, I thank you for lifting me when I'm weak, giving me strength when I'm strengthless, and leading me when I don't want to be led. Thank you for the courage to press, even when I'm confused, burnt out, tired, and stressed.

I surrender my financial concerns to you, every debt, every fear, and every doubt. I choose to cast my burdens upon you, knowing you care deeply for me. I release my desire to control; I trust in your timing and provision. Lord, you know best what I need.

As I enter this transition, thank you for a transformation in my finances, heart, and mindset. Thank you for teaching me to walk in faith, believing in your abundance rather than my abilities. Align my desires with your purpose and thank you for giving me wisdom and integrity to steward the blessings you have entrusted to me.

I declare that these days will be a turning point in my life. I am grateful that you reveal what is already mine, even things I do not yet know. As you said in 1 Corinthians 2:9, you have prepared blessings beyond anything I have seen, heard, or conceived. Thank you, Lord, for all that awaits. I step into this journey with hope, faith, and a spirit of expectancy. In Jesus' name, Amen.

Meditation Scriptures

- Romans 5:2
- Genesis 12:1-3
- 1 Corinthians 2:9

Reflection Questions

1. What financial breakthroughs are you expecting God to work in your life over these fourteen days?

2. What answered prayers are you currently living in?

3. How can you cultivate gratitude in your daily financial habits?

Notes

DAY 2

LET IT GO: FORGIVENESS FOR FREEDOM

"Bearing with one another and, if one has a complaint against another, forgiving each other; as the Lord has forgiven you, so you also must forgive."
~ Colossians 3:13

To say I questioned God a million times would still be putting it lightly. Growing up, I knew deep down that I was meant for more than what I saw around me. I recognized my identity in God but wasn't in an environment that nurtured it. I carried bitterness, felt shame more times than I'd like to admit, and blamed myself for not having the right mindset to make different choices. Those limiting beliefs followed me into adulthood, causing me to pass on opportunities that would grow me financially, professionally, and personally because they seemed "too big" or beyond what my mind could conceive.

While I'm in an okay place today and "okay" is relative, depending on whom you ask, I've realized there's still some unforgiveness I've been holding on to. Forgiveness is not always about forgiving others; sometimes, it's about forgiving yourself for the choices you made or didn't make.

I often remember having an incredible opportunity to move to Boston, Massachusetts, to work for GE. The recruiter was relentless, reaching out to me for a week straight, even contacting the admissions office to track me down and let me know that I was the perfect fit and that the job was mine. And what did I do? I cried, and they weren't tears of joy but tears of worry, not feeling like I was enough, and ultimately, tears of fear. I was terrified of the unknown and overwhelmed by the thought of stepping into something that felt much bigger than me. What if I fail? What if I don't belong?

At that moment, I let fear decide for me. I told myself that staying in my comfort zone and leaving my small town was okay. Staying within a few hours felt manageable. But leaving the state? That was a different ballgame, one I hadn't signed up for.

Now, I wonder what life might have looked like if I hadn't been so afraid. While that opportunity maybe wasn't meant for me, I'll never know because I let fear of the unknown stop me before I even tried. Don't get it twisted; this day is still about forgiveness. While it may sound like it's moved to talking about overcoming fear, trust me, we'll get there. But do you see how all these struggles are tied together? Looking back, I've realized that when we carry around many "what could have been" and "what should have been," it's usually a sign that we're holding unforgiveness, even toward ourselves.

But it's time to forgive myself for that decision. Oh, and did I mention the starting salary in 2009 was six figures? Yeah, that part stings a little. But today isn't about holding on to those regrets but letting them go. I'm choosing to forgive myself for being afraid of change, letting fear dictate my choices, and doubting my ability to handle God's offer.

Before we can build something new in our financial lives, we must clear away the debris of old hurts, shame, and regret. The prayer you're about to read is an honest conversation with God, asking Him to forgive you and intentionally choosing to forgive yourself and others. It's about releasing the weight of the past and stepping into the freedom, healing, and possibility that He so freely offers.

Forgiveness isn't just a one-time deal; it's an ongoing door opening us up to healing, fresh opportunities, and a future shaped by God's abundant promises rather than our old mistakes.

Prayer

God,

Forgive me for my sins, those I knew I was committing, and those I committed blindly. Forgive me for not trusting you when all the signs pointed to me needing to trust you. God, forgive me for making my path. Although seemingly good at the time, I went independent of your word and ignored your directions.

You came to free me from guilt, so I let go of the burden. Right now, I reclaim my life, placing you at the head of it all. Thank you for carrying me and never changing who you are. Forgive me for acting as though you shifted with my circumstances.

I release every heavy chain pulling me backward: old beliefs, shameful secrets, and unresolved relationships, and I let go of the guilt tied to my past. These choices don't define my worth; they remind me that I'm human. The enemy no longer gets to hold my past over my head. I give it to you, Jesus, and take back the authority you gave me.

I forgive the people in my past and present: parents, spouses, exes, friends, and anyone connected to my financial pain. Forgive me for being angry that things weren't different, for resenting decisions I had no control over, or for the times I lacked necessities. For the times I looked at my counterparts and wished that was me, wondering and settling on the fact that you'd forgotten about me. For the times when the electricity had to go off, I had to scrape together food, or I felt I reached my lowest point. God, I release that anger now.

My past isn't my future; I take back my freedom and my mindset. Today, I take control and accept all you have for me. Today, I accept your freedom and let go, moving forward with the confidence that I am not meant to be poor, timid, or broken. Forgive me for living with a poverty mindset, wrongfully acting like it was the best YOU could do. Help me to walk in forgiveness and to live in the forgiveness that you have given me.

I am not blaming credit card companies, marketers, social media, or flashy lifestyles. I admit that sometimes I've chosen to keep up rather than look up to you, the one who keeps me secure. Forgive me for chasing after every quick fix, every new gimmick, and scheme without seeking your guidance first. Forgive me for failing to see you as my trustworthy provider.

God, you promised that you would never leave or forsake me; you said that you supply every one of my needs according to your riches in glory in Christ Jesus. You are my Father, and I can't even put your riches and wealth into numbers, which means I have access to anything & everything I need. God, you gave your only Son, which means nothing according to your will is off-limits. Help me to remember that everything I need is in you. Forgive me for seeing you as limited or unreachable.

And Lord, even as I experience stability, comfort, and abundance, forgive me for the times I've closed my hands and hardened my heart. Lord, forgive me for even the bitterness that I hold that may have pushed me to create the lifestyle I live. I confess I've sometimes relied on the safety of my provision instead of seeking your guidance and direction for how to use it. Forgive me for clinging to what you've so generously given instead of pouring it out into the lives of others. Teach me to be open-handed, generous, and willing to invest in Kingdom purposes, reminding me that every good thing I have comes from you.

I will no longer settle for a lesser or different version of the life you've promised me. In Jesus' Name, Amen.

Meditation Scriptures

- Ephesians 4:32
- Matthew 6:14-15

Reflection Questions

1. What financial regrets or sources of shame have you been carrying? How can you release them to God today?

2. Whom must you forgive (family, friends, or even yourself) for past financial mistakes or hurts?

3. In what ways have you seen God's faithfulness, even when you felt you were at fault or undeserving?

Notes

DAY 3

ALIGNING BELIEF & MINDSET

"For as he thinketh in his heart, so is he: Eat and drink, saith he to thee; but his heart is not with thee." ~ Proverbs 23:7

Let's clarify one thing: nothing in Scripture suggests that the God of love wants His people to live broke, busted, or disgusted (there, I said it). In fact, the Bible tells us that He gives us the power to get wealth. The passage in 1 Timothy 6, which we often misquote, wasn't written to condemn having money; it was written to encourage Godly living and warn against the snares of evil and temptation; one potential evil being the misuse of money. Timothy's point was to keep God at the center, so wealth doesn't become a stumbling block.

Not everyone with money falls into temptation. Timothy shows us how our attitude toward money and our walk with God are linked. Money itself isn't evil, but the excessive craving for it is. If you read further, verse 17 acknowledges that some believers will be rich. So, what's the advice? Wealthy people are instructed not to be arrogant or trust in their wealth, as it can vanish anytime. Instead, they should trust in God, who blesses us generously and use their resources to do good, help others, and live open-handedly. By doing so, they store up treasures that truly matter.

This connects directly to the authority and dominion God grants us and the authority I've used to command my mind to align with where God is taking me. Has it been easy? Absolutely not, and if I'm honest, I've wanted to quit pursuing the "Shavonna" God sees me as; the person I think is sometimes over the top, quite "bougie," having high standards. But there was a deeper and different place God was calling me for the sake of others, and I had two choices: believe Him or not. Once I chose belief, I stopped hiding my blessings, feeling guilty about them, and being ashamed of what God had done in my life.

God spoke to me and said: "You're struggling with who you left behind: family, coworkers, and business partners. You diminish your blessings as if my promises aren't a big deal, as if living your best life doesn't matter. You belittle my promises by attaching a "that old thing" decal to it. But that ends now. In this season, you must acknowledge that I've kept my promises. People around you struggle and need a sign that I'm still working miracles. That sign comes from you. When they see you happy, they'll say, 'If He did it for her, He can do it for me.' I will use the promises I kept in your life to restore someone else's faith."

He reminded me that His favor is on me, His word is deep in my heart, and that if I remember Him, He will keep blessing me. Because I'm openly living a blessed life, people will recognize the anointing on and in me. They'll see I'm not perfect but connected to

Him, which makes the difference. My life is an example of not being religious but having a relationship with Him.

God explained that people will wonder, "What does she do?" which is exactly why He allowed all I went through: my upbringing, heartaches, and disappointments (we'll save that for another book). People needed to see how it started so they could witness His grace at work. Like Sarah waiting on her promise until it seemed impossible, God waited until I was on the other side of "impossible" so everyone could know His promises are possible.

Can we say mic drop? At that moment, it hit me: one of the enemy's greatest tactics is to distort our mindset about wealth, provision, and money. If he can make us question the legitimate promises of God, you know, the ones that come without sorrow (Proverbs 10:22), the answered prayers, and the light that shines through our happiness, he's completed his job of defeat. If that isn't enough, he makes us feel guilty about what we have, who we were required to leave behind, and all that God can and wants to do for us. The enemy's job is to make "struggle" and "poverty gospel" seem noble or attractive, leaving us tangled in this web of regret, jealousy, brokenness, and joylessness. Ultimately, this leads us to covet what others have, doubt our worth, and feel like we'll never be enough or have enough. Talk about a lie! All while serving a God we know to be more than enough.

But here's the thing, stewardship starts in the mind. When we know our identity as His children, we use the power Christ has given us to live out our purpose. Our beliefs shape our reality, and our mindset influences how we respond to challenges and opportunities, even when it comes directly from the mouth of God. Today, choose to release any negative views about money, shame, guilt, the endless opportunities and places God has called you to, and embrace a Kingdom mindset built on abundance and stewardship. Aligning your thoughts with God's word and his vision for you, no matter how big and scary it is, produces true financial transformation.

Prayer

Faithful Father,

I thank you for your word, which is alive and active, sharper than any two-edged sword. Your truth is the light that casts out the shadows of doubt, fear, and lack. Lord, today I ask you to help me align my thoughts with your truth. I surrender every limiting belief, every lie of insufficiency, and every fear about my finances to you. Renew my mind, Lord, so that I may see my circumstances through the lens of your abundance and faithfulness.

Your word declares that as a man thinks in his heart, so is he. I reject thoughts of scarcity, shame, and guilt and choose to embrace the mindset of a faithful steward, knowing that you have given me the ability to create wealth and prosper for your glory. Help me to see money as a tool, not a master, and to trust in you as my ultimate source rather than the works of my hands.

As I align my beliefs with your truth, Lord, help me to remember the authority and dominion you have granted me as a part of Christ's body (Ephesians 1:19-23). Seated with Him above every form of wickedness, I carry through the Holy Spirit an immeasurable power that the enemy can never surpass. While material wealth itself is not evil, after all, even Abraham was richly blessed (Genesis 13:2); it's the LOVE of money that leads hearts astray (1 Timothy 6:10). Instead, let me pursue the type of prosperity that reflects true Kingdom values, wisdom, righteousness (Proverbs 8:9), and a deep, abiding relationship with you. Remind me daily that my connection with you is more valuable than any possession, and that walking in my God-given dominion means keeping you at the center of everything I do.

Father, I ask for your wisdom to guard my mind against worldly patterns of greed, fear, or comparison. Teach me to meditate on your promises, to declare your word over my finances, and to walk in obedience to your instructions. Just as you spoke to Joshua, I choose to be strong and courageous, meditating on your law, day and night so that I may be careful to do everything written in it and prosper wherever I go.

Lord, I believe in the plans you have for me. Plans to prosper me and not to harm me, plans to give me a hope and a future (Jeremiah 29:11). I cast down every imagination and argument that exalts itself against the knowledge of you, bringing every thought into captivity to the obedience of Christ. Transform my mindset so that I can walk **confidently** in your provision.

Thank you for being my shepherd and my provider. I trust you to align my heart, my mind, and my actions with your Kingdom principles. In Jesus' name, Amen.

Meditation Scriptures

- Romans 12:2
- Philippians 4:8
- 2 Corinthians 10:5

Reflection Questions

1. What negative beliefs about money do you need to surrender to God?

____

____

____

____

____

____

____

____

2. How can you replace those beliefs with truths from God's word?

____

____

____

____

____

____

____

____

3. What practical steps can you take to align your financial habits with a Kingdom mindset?

____

____

____

____

____

____

____

Notes

DAY 4

WRITE IT DOWN, WATCH IT HAPPEN

The Lord answered me and said, "Write the vision and make it plain upon tablets, that he may run that readeth it." ~ Habakkuk 2:2

I remember one morning sitting and praying, seeking God about His vision and promises for my life. If I'm honest, the math wasn't mathin' for me. I was really frustrated with where we were in our finances. Additionally, I didn't feel like my business was going in the direction it should've been, and I was frustrated, very frustrated (did I say frustrated?). I began asking God to show me where He was taking me, where His word, my wealth, and His transformation in the hearts of his people would align.

In one voice, this man (God), without hesitation, whispered to me, "Talk Show." I laughed hysterically (I am still working through those limiting beliefs), got up, and told myself to get out of my head. At that point, I knew I had done something wrong, wandering out of God's presence and onto the set of my favorite talk show. I even asked for forgiveness for not staying focused during a serious time. Needless to say, I pulled a Sarah when God told her she would bear a child in her old age. I even texted a team member because that's how "crazy" I felt. My exact words to her were, "I asked the Lord to show me the ideas that will lead to my money, and I heard talk show... I'm like, dude, really".

But I hope you know that God gets the last laugh. Not even five hours later, God led a prophet (who was a stranger) to me, who called me out of 700+ women to tell me many things (including this devotional being produced) and to say to me, "You're a modern-day Joseph whom God has shown how to deal with finances. I don't know what you're doing, but I see something that looks like a talk show, a TV show." STOP THE PRESS!! If you know me, I lost it as soon as she said talk show. Like wailing, not even crying anymore. So, if your mind is blown, mine is still blown a year later. I am telling you this for a few reasons:

- God's vision is always bigger and scarier than anything we can imagine.

- **God's vision for you, spoken through someone else should be confirmation from your prayer and personal time with him.**

- It hasn't happened as of the time I'm writing this devotional, but me writing it in this book for millions (yes, millions - you see what I did there?) to read forces me to "write it" and commit to it.

God often shows us visions that challenge our current understanding and comfort zones, showing possibilities far beyond our abilities. These visions can feel scary because they stretch our faith, requiring us to trust His strength rather than our limited resources. Yet, Scripture consistently reminds us that God has not called us to live in fear. Passages like 2 Timothy 1:7 assure us that He has given us a spirit of power, love, and a sound mind, not a spirit of fear.

Similarly, throughout the Bible, God instructs His people not to be afraid because He is with them (Isaiah 41:10). In other words, the vision may be intimidating, but we are never alone; we can move forward with courage, knowing that the One who gave the vision also promises His presence, guidance, and 24/7 support. God calls us to live with intentionality and purpose. Writing down your financial goals and dreams is an act of faith that displays your trust in God's promises. Today, we focus on clarifying our vision, writing it down and trusting that it will come to pass in His perfect timing.

Prayer

God of More,

I thank you for being a God of clarity and purpose. You have called me to live a life of meaning and placed dreams and desires in my heart. Just as you instructed the prophet Habakkuk to write the vision and make it plain so that others may run with it, I take this step of faith today to write down the vision you have given me for my finances.

Lord, I ask for your guidance as I clarify my goals. Show me what aligns with your will and purpose for my life. Help me to dream boldly and trust in your ability to provide beyond what I can ask or imagine, as your word promises in Ephesians 3:20.

Father, I know that visions take time to unfold, and I ask for patience and trust in your timing. Teach me to persevere and remain steadfast, even when nothing is happening. Your word reminds me that the vision awaits an appointed time; it will not delay. I choose to wait with expectancy, knowing that you are faithful in completing the good work you have begun in me.

Thank you, Lord, for the resources, ideas, and strategies you're providing to help me accomplish the vision. May my financial goals not only bless me but also advance your Kingdom and testify to your goodness. Lord, I humbly ask for revelation for the next steps. I trust in you completely. In Jesus' name, Amen.

Meditation Scriptures

- Habakkuk 2:2-3
- Proverbs 16:3
- Jeremiah 29:11
- Isaiah 41:10

Reflection Questions

1. What financial dreams or goals has God placed on your heart? Have you written these dreams down? If not, take time to do so today.

2. How can you ensure your financial vision aligns with God's Kingdom purpose?

Notes

DAY 5

TRUST GOD'S TIMING

"But do not overlook this one fact, beloved, that with the Lord, one day is as a thousand years and a thousand years as one day. The Lord is not slow to fulfill his promise as some count slowness but is patient toward you, not wishing that any should perish, but that all should reach repentance."

~ 2 Peter 3:8-9

"If Only You Will Trust Me" isn't just a melody; it's a phrase the Father often whispers to my ears. I remember sitting down and praying what I call a "Solomon prayer": "Here I am, God, right in the middle of the people you've chosen, so numerous I couldn't count them." But then I added, "Lord, it's not looking like what you promised." I was in a place where I needed answers, but I also needed to increase my seek (i.e., prayer time) to understand his timing.

It's not ironic that this topic comes after writing and accepting the vision. I was frank with God, admitting that I felt like I'd move two steps forward only to get pushed ten steps back. Once I finally aligned with the vision, prophecy, and this big, scary future He showed me, nothing seemed to match the timing as I thought it would. Seriously,

God, where is the multi-million-dollar contract for the talk show? At this point, I can barely get past 100 views on YouTube. However, during prayer, I was reminded to believe. Not to grow discouraged because I was on the verge of a breakthrough, but I must remain **consistent** to see the fruit of my labor. It wasn't here yet, but when it arrived, I would know.

But here's what I've come to realize: trusting God's timing still requires our participation. It's not passive. It's not just sitting back and waiting. Trusting Him demands consistency even when nothing around you makes sense. It requires prayer so you can discern when God is saying "pivot" versus when the enemy is trying to distract you. It demands focus KNOWING chaos will come. Without that focus, your mind becomes a playground for the enemy, planting lies and doubt.

While "trust" is a simple five-letter word, it's one of the biggest hurdles we face as believers. Trust is where what we say we believe meets how we live. It's where our lips and our hearts finally align. And when they do, our praise becomes deeper, our faith becomes louder, and God becomes delighted in our dependence on Him as both sustainer and provider. No, He didn't promise it would be easy, but He did promise His plans are good and never to harm us (Jeremiah 29:11).

The truth is, when we look back, we should often thank God for not answering our prayers exactly when we wanted Him to do so. Imagine how badly we would've handled it if He had given us what we asked for too soon. When our mindsets were off, our hearts were heavy with unforgiveness, we lacked gratitude, and our vision was blurry. Waiting on God can be one of the most complex and sometimes frustrating parts of the faith journey, but His timing is perfect. Like a farmer who plants seeds, patiently waiting for the harvest, we must trust God's process and realize delays aren't denials. Today, let's focus on staying steadfast in faith, holding firm to God's divine timing for our financial breakthroughs.

Prayer

God of Perfect Timing,

I come before you with a heart that longs to trust you more. Lord, I acknowledge that your ways and thoughts are higher than mine. Even when I cannot see the whole picture, I trust that you are working behind the scenes, orchestrating every detail for my good and your glory.

Father, your word reminds me in Habakkuk 2:3 that the vision is for an appointed time. Though it may linger, I will wait for it, for it will certainly come and not be delayed. Help me to remain steadfast in faith, holding onto your promises even when my circumstances seem unchanged. Teach me to rest in the assurance that you are always on time, never too early, and never too late.

Lord, I admit that waiting is hard. There are moments when doubt creeps in and whispers that nothing will change. In those moments, strengthen my heart and remind me of your faithfulness. As Galatians 6:9 encourages, I will not grow weary in doing well; at the proper time, I will reap a harvest if I do not give in.

Father, I thank you for the lessons that come in the waiting. You are refining me, building my character, and preparing me for the blessings you have in store. Help me trust that every delay is part of your perfect plan. May I use my waiting seasons to grow closer to you, deepen my faith, and steward what you have given me well.

Lord, I surrender my timeline to you and trust in yours. Grant me the strength to stay consistent and steadfast. I will not waver in my position, for I know my labor in you is not in vain. Thank you for being a God who sees the end from the beginning and always fulfills His promises. I place my life in your hands, confident that you will bring everything to pass at the right time. In Jesus' name, Amen.

Meditation Scriptures

- Proverbs 3:5-6
- Isaiah 40:31
- Lamentations 3:25-26
- Psalms 27:14

Reflection Questions

1. Reflect on a time when God's timing proved perfect in your life. How does this encourage you now?

____

____

____

____

____

____

____

2. Are there any financial concerns you need to surrender control and trust God's process?

____

____

____

____

____

____

____

Notes

DAY 6

THE HEART BEHIND THE GIFT

"But remember the Lord your God, for it is He who gives you the ability to produce wealth, and so confirms His covenant, which He swore to your ancestors, as it is today." ~ Deuteronomy 8:18

Let's talk about giving and not just tithing, not just the 10%, but a heart that's postured to honor God with all that you have. Let's go ahead and talk about the part most people avoid. That awkward responsibility, especially when your bank account is low, your bills are high, or you've just don't feel the need. However, if we're going to discuss financial transformation, walking in God's promises, and truly living free in faith and finances, we cannot skip over this.

Giving is one of those spiritual principles we love to receive the fruit of but sometimes hesitate to participate in. Especially when finances feel tight, or life feels uncertain. But here's what I've learned: giving is not about an amount; it's about alignment. It's about the posture of your heart toward God and your willingness to let go of what He's entrusted to you, knowing He has even more. Because the truth is, overlooking the requirement to give voids every promise written in this devotional. God doesn't need your money, but your willingness to give reveals something deeper: your obedience, your love, and your trust. God didn't stutter in Malachi 3:10: "Bring the whole tithe into the storehouse, that there may be food in my house. **Test** me in this," says the Lord Almighty, "and see if I will not throw open the floodgates of heaven and pour out so much blessing that there will not be room enough to store it."

Let's pause. God literally says test me. The Creator of Heaven and Earth is permitting us to test His faithfulness by giving back a portion of what He gave us to begin with (knowing he's going to win). And somehow, we still wrestle with it. Why? Because it's not really about the money, it's about the heart. **Giving is not a money problem; it's a trust issue.**

We're okay trusting God with our healing, our protection, and even our families. But our wallets? That's where we start giving Him conditions. "Lord, when I earn a little more, I'll give" or "Once I pay off this debt, I'll start giving." But obedience doesn't wait for you to be ready to surrender.

Giving Illustrates Three Things:

1. Obedience

God's Word is clear. We, as believers, are called to give. Not to take from us but to bless us. Not out of pressure but out of purpose. Luke

6:38 says, "Give, and it will be given to you… For with the measure you use, it will be measured to you." This isn't prosperity gimmickry; it's a kingdom principle. Giving unlocks doors because it proves you're in tune with God's will, not just your desires.

2. Love

When we give, we're saying, "God, I love You more than I love what You've given me." John 14:15 says, "If you love me, keep my commandments." Love is not just warm feelings or emotional experiences; it's shown in action. Giving is one of the clearest ways we express our love for God. When we love someone, we want to please them, serve them, and prioritize what matters to them. God's heart is for His people, His church, and His Kingdom. So, when we give, we're making our love for Him greater than our money. Our love displays our desire to partner with Him in meeting needs and spreading His Word.

3. Trust

Giving forces you to lean on God. It reveals where your trust really lies. It's an act of faith that says, "Lord, You're my source. My job, my savings, my account balance, those are resources, but you are the source." And when we release our grip, God reveals His. The amount we give isn't a tax; it's a **trust test**. Proverbs 3:5 tells us to "trust in the Lord with all your heart and lean not on your own understanding."

That includes trusting Him with your money. When you give, especially when it's tight, inconvenient, or sacrificial, you're declaring that you trust that He can do above and beyond what your obedience could ever do. It's you saying, "God, I believe you'll do more with my 90% than I ever could with the whole 100%." It's not about what leaves your hand; it's about what that surrender invites into your life

Let's be real. We are human, and I would be lying if I said I always gave with ease. There were seasons I gave out of obligation, not understanding. I've had seasons where giving was easy and seasons where it took everything in me to sow a seed. Sometimes, I gave in faith; other times, I gave with fear and doubt whispering in my ear. But looking back, the moments that stretched me the most were the moments that changed me the most. And as you can imagine, there was never a time God didn't provide and never a time He didn't multiply.

Giving isn't about being flashy. It's not about providing big numbers. It's about letting your generosity align with your gratitude. And yes, while tithing is a biblical standard (Malachi 3:10), this chapter isn't just about the 10%. It's about the heart of a giver. Being a cheerful giver opened doors I didn't even think to pray for: unexpected checks in the mail, supernatural favor, and provisions that didn't make sense on paper. It wasn't magic or luck; it was God's promise in action.

But let me be clear: **Giving doesn't buy your way into Heaven**. Let's cancel that theology right now. You can't throw a few dollars at the altar and think it earns your righteousness. You still need a relationship with the Father. You still need obedience, humility, and a surrendered heart.

Look at the Israelites. What should've taken them 11 days took 40 years. Why? Because of disobedience. They wanted the promise but not the process. They wanted provision without submission. And I don't want that for you. Giving and tithing is part of your walk. It's not optional; it's foundational. And it doesn't matter if you make $100 or $10,000 a month. The same principle applies. If you can't give now, you won't suddenly start when you make more.

You can read this whole devotional, pray every prayer, and quote every scripture, but if your heart is closed to giving, it short-circuits the power of what God wants to do through you. When we hold back, it's not just our bank accounts that suffer; it's our growth, our witness, and our capacity to steward more. God wants to bless you, but not just for you. Sowing into good ground supports your church, feeds others, carries the gospel, funds outreach, builds safe spaces, and, yes, advances the Kingdom.

It's not about guilt; it's about grace. You give because He gave. You bless others because you've been blessed. And even when it's hard, you sow because you trust that He's faithful to bring the harvest.

Giving is not something you do when you have extra; it's something that you do because you serve an extra God in every aspect of the Word. He is extra faithful, extra generous, and extra good. Giving does not take from you; it frees you. It breaks the grip of greed, fear, and control. It's how we say thank you to a faithful God, not only with our lips but our heart.

And if you absolutely want to walk with me on this faith and finance journey, giving can't be an option. It's a way of life. A declaration. A reminder that you live with your hands open, ready to receive, but always open to let go.

Prayer

El Shaddai,

Thank you for being the ultimate giver. You give me life, you give me strength, and most of all, you gave Your Son so I could be reconciled back to you. Lord, I admit there have been times when I've held tightly to what's in my hand. There were times when fear, lack, or doubt made me question if I had enough to give. But today, I choose to realign my heart.

Father, remind me that it is not the quantity that counts but where my heart stands. Teach me to give out of a heart of obedience, showing that I love you more than I love money, and out of a heart of trust, knowing that you are my Source and all else is merely a resource. Teach me to see giving as worship, not as drudgery, and allow my giving to reflect your faithfulness in my life.

God, I ask that you break every fear or scarcity mindset that keeps me from releasing what belongs to you. Shift my perspective so I see giving not as losing but as planting: planting into your Kingdom, planting into others' lives, and planting into the future you've promised me. I believe, Lord, that you will multiply what I sow, not for my glory but so I can continue to be a blessing to others.

Guard my heart from selfishness, greed, and comparison. Please fill me with joy and cheerfulness as I give, even in moments when it stretches me. And let my life be a living testimony that when I honor you first, you open the windows of heaven and pour out blessings I cannot contain.

I surrender my finances to you, Lord. Take my tithe, my offering, my giving, rather large or small, and use it for your glory. And as I walk this journey of faith and finances, help me always to keep my heart behind the gift pure, grateful, and surrendered. In Jesus' name, Amen.

Meditation Scriptures

- Malachi 3:10
- Proverbs 3:9–10
- 2 Corinthians 9:6–7
- Luke 6:38
- Deuteronomy 8:18

Reflection Questions

1. What areas of your finances are you still trying to control instead of trusting God with? Why is it hard to release?

2. What's one fear or limiting belief you have about giving that you need to lay at God's feet today?

3. In what ways has God shown Himself faithful when you chose to give, even when you weren't sure how things would work out? Did you take time to truly recognize that moment as God's provision?

Notes

DAY 7
EMBRACING STEWARDSHIP

"His master replied, 'Well done, good and faithful servant! You have been faithful with a few things; I will put you in charge of many things. Come and share your master's happiness!" ~ Matthew 25:23

Most people hear "stewardship" and immediately think it's about money. And yes, God has absolutely called us to steward our finances wisely, but that's just one piece of the puzzle. Stewardship includes more than just budgets and bank accounts. It's about mission and vision: using the resources God has temporarily placed under your care to further His purpose in the world and fulfill His vision.

Let's be honest, though; stewardship of our finances is hard, or I should say we make it hard. Stewardship is a big word for something simple: managing what you've been given well. With respect to your finances, it's choosing responsibility over impulse. It's making wise decisions, resisting the urge to buy something for temporary joy and realizing that just because you can afford it doesn't mean you need it (delayed gratification). Essentially, stewardship is obedience.

There was a moment when my husband and I felt stuck in our finances. (Yes, again, I told you, this is a journey, not a destination!) We were doing okay; we had food on the table, the lights stayed on, and we paid all our bills. But we weren't growing. We had become comfortable with the money being there. We stopped setting goals and began pulling from our savings and investments more often than adding to them.

The real gut punch came the following year when we did our taxes. It wasn't until that moment that we realized that the previous year, we had experienced an influx of income like we'd never seen before. A year that couldn't be explained except by God's favor. It was the kind of year where we could've hired a butler for fun. And yet, when we looked back, we realized we didn't have much growth to show for it. Sure, we managed to keep the bills paid, but we hadn't demonstrated to God that we could handle what He'd graciously trusted us with.

I imagined God saying, "Let's slow this train down." And He did just that. That following year looked nothing like the previous one. At that moment, we knew we'd dropped the ball. Everything we taught about stewardship and management. We had failed the test. It was humbling, but it was also a painful wake-up call. We updated our budget, rededicated our accounts back to God, started having intentional conversations about where every dollar was going before it hit our bank account, and got serious (again) about honoring God with our resources. While it stung us to face our mistakes, it taught us an invaluable truth: stewardship and management are the keys to sustaining wealth. More than that, stewardship is an act of worship, worship through gratitude.

As parents, we understand this on a human level. We know which of our kids can be trusted with more and which ones need a tighter leash. If you suddenly became a billionaire, you already know which child you could trust with a $50,000 monthly allowance and which might blow $50,000 daily. It's the same with God. He's not broke; He's looking for stewards He can trust.

Today, let's align our financial decisions with God's principles, make room for His blessings, and commit to walking according to His will. Stewardship is not just a responsibility; it's an opportunity to reflect His goodness and honor Him in all we do.

Prayer

Heavenly Father,

Thank you for entrusting me with the resources you have placed in my hands. I acknowledge that everything I have comes from you, for your word declares in Psalm 24:1 that the earth and everything in it belong to you. I am simply a steward of what you have given me, and I desire to honor you with my stewardship.

Lord, I ask for your guidance and wisdom in managing the blessings you have provided me. Help me make decisions that reflect your

Kingdom principles, not my desires. Teach me to be faithful with little so you may trust me with more, as Luke 16:10 promises.

Father, I want to honor you in every aspect of my finances. Help me to create a budget that reflects my priorities and aligns with your will. Give me discipline to stay on track and generosity to bless others. Let my financial choices reflect my faith and trust in you, knowing that as I give, it will be given back to me, pressed down, shaken together, and running over, as Luke 6:38 teaches.

Lord, I also pray for a heart of gratitude and contentment. In a world that constantly pushes for more, help me to find joy in what you have already provided. Let me remember that true wealth is found in living according to your purpose and fulfilling the plans you have for me.

Father, I declare today that I will walk in obedience to your word, trusting that as I seek first your Kingdom and righteousness, all things will be added to me. Thank you for being my Provider, my Guide, and my Source. I commit to being a faithful steward of all you have given me. In Jesus' name, Amen.

Meditation Scriptures

- Luke 16:10
- Proverbs 21:20
- Psalms 24:1

Reflection Questions

1. What does faithful stewardship look like in your current season of life?

2. Are there areas in your life where you need to practice greater financial discipline?

Notes

DAY 8

FEAR IS NOT YOUR FUTURE

"Fear not, for I am with you; be not dismayed, for I am your God; I will strengthen you, I will help you, I will uphold you with my righteous right hand." ~ Isaiah 41:10

Fear is one of the enemy's easiest weapons to use against us. Fear of the unknown, loss, change, failure; these feelings all funnel down to the same anxious question: "What if?" Fear is worrying about something that hasn't happened yet, as if we have a superpower to predict disaster and failure. For some of us, this superpower is broken because we see failure in everything. While I am being facetious, we are not God, so why do we move through life like failure is the only outcome?

Some of you know my story: I'm a certified wedding and event planner. Planning experiences that help women evolve and grow in God has always been part of my "why." In 2023, I hosted an incredible event called the "Pink Pajama Brunch," which carried such a powerful, God-given anointing. It was one of those events where you left drained and empty, not in a bad way, but a moment where God pulled everything out of you while finding a way to feel you back up. Tears of joy flowed down my face for most of the event. Although beautiful, intimate, and powerful, I feared recreating it. I've been terrified that I'd never measure up to that special moment again, to the glory and presence that filled the room.

Five days before the event, during one of the most challenging seasons in life **EVER**, God nudged me mid-flight to write a personal, prophetic word for each guest. I was drained emotionally, physically, and spiritually. So, of course, I pushed back with all the excuses: "I'm too tired, I don't know everyone, and this is last-minute." But I obeyed. That simple act of obedience changed lives; people walked away with freedom, answers, and joy. Some stop me even now to let me know they carry their cards, turning to them when life gets hard.

You'd think this cheerful story ends with me putting the enemy in his place and telling you how I didn't allow fear to step in the way of continuing and walking in purpose. But here I am, a year later, although I've been asked when the next one will occur, I haven't made any effort to take this to the next level or plan the next brunch experience. After writing this, though, I'm determined not to let fear rob others of their breakthrough ever again.

I must remind myself not to give fear of change more power than fear of staying stuck.

Even when it's big, scary, and out of my comfort zone, I won't let fear hold me back. A random social media post hit home: "The enemy wants to trap you in fear, keep you stuck in the battle, and feed you lies because something significant is being birthed as you lean into God." That's exactly what my brand aims to do! Help women push past uncertainty and fear in their finances and sense of self-worth.

If I'm completely honest, sometimes we fear that God might fail us. Some might call that thought outrageous, but how many backup plans have we made, even after God has told us to stand still and trust Him? Fear paralyzes us, especially in our finances, turning a temporary dilemma into a permanent destiny. But fear doesn't define our future. Today, we're choosing to break free from fear and embrace the courage and confidence from God's presence. As I write this, "Fear Is Not My Future" by Todd Galberth feat. Tasha Cobb is ministering to me. A timely reminder that fear isn't allowed to commune with you.

Prayer

Mighty Warrior,

I praise you for being my refuge, strength, and ever-present help in times of trouble. You are the God who goes before me, the One who fights my battles, and the One who upholds me with your righteous right hand. Because you are with me, I will not be afraid.

Lord, I bring every fear and anxiety about my finances before you. Fear of lack, failure, and the unknown—I lay them all at your feet. Your word reminds me in Joshua 1:9 to be strong and courageous, not afraid or discouraged, for you are with me wherever I go. Please help me hold onto this truth when fear overwhelms me.

Father, your perfect love casts out all fear. Fill me with your love today, saturating every corner of my heart so that fear has no room to dwell. Remind me that you have not given me a spirit of fear but power, love, and a sound mind. I choose to walk in the authority you gave me, declaring that fear has no hold over my life or finances.

Lord, I ask for boldness to take steps of faith even when the path is unclear. Like Joshua leading the Israelites into the Promised Land, I will trust in your presence and strength to guide me. Fear will not dictate my decisions or my destiny.

Thank you, Lord, for being my peace in the storm and light in the darkness. I trust you to provide, protect, and lead me every step of the way. Thank you, Lord, for all that awaits. It's a new day, and I choose to rejoice in the new me. In Jesus' name, Amen

Meditation Scriptures

- 2 Timothy 1:7
- Isaiah 41:10
- Joshua 1:9
- Psalms 34:4

Reflection Questions

1. What financial fears do you need to face?

2. How does God's words reassure you when fear begins to creep in?

3. Are there specific situations where you need to take a step of faith despite fear?

Notes

DAY 9

WALK IT OUT (FINANCIAL CONFIDENCE)

"Let us then approach God's throne of grace with confidence, so that we may receive mercy and find grace to help us in our time of need." ~ Hebrews 4:16

Confidence is the belief in YOUR abilities and decisions. It assures you that you can effectively handle tasks, make decisions, and overcome obstacles. In money management, confidence means trusting your financial knowledge and skills, enabling you to manage your resources wisely. Being financially confident ultimately means having clarity, control, and peace of mind over your financial life. Financial confidence isn't about having it all figured out or reaching a particular income level; it's about building a solid foundation that allows you to handle challenges, seize opportunities, and feel secure in the path you're creating.

Life events and circumstances play a significant role in your confidence. Positive moments, like career advancements or financial wins, can make you feel unstoppable, while setbacks like job loss or financial struggles can leave you doubtful in your decisions. But here's the truth: maintaining confidence requires more than external wins. It takes resilience and, most importantly, a foundation deeply rooted in God. Here's the thing, if your confidence isn't grounded in Him, the enemy will use every opportunity to let the timid, indecisive version of you take center stage. He'll twist those indecisive doubts into your identity, making you believe that's who you are. But that's a lie, and it's time to call it out.

Confidence in any area of life starts with believing that God can and will. Yet, when making life-changing decisions, whether in your family, marriage, career, or finances, people often jump straight into action without addressing what's happening in their hearts and minds. And that's where you go wrong. Instead of building lasting solutions, you create temporary fixes that fail to produce the dreams and goals you long for. Why? Because your confidence isn't grounded in the one place it needs to be: in God. To handle what He's doing and where He's taking you, your confidence will keep you from wavering when, to the world, it doesn't make sense. You must be confident before you take action!

Every decision in your heart should align with your belief in Him. When you're standing on His word and letting Him direct your steps, you can trust yourself to make the right financial and life decisions. And when you trust in Him, you'll start to see His promises come to life.

Lasting results and true change flow from confident decisions. Confident decisions come from believing in yourself. Believing in yourself comes from having confidence in God. And confidence in

God comes from a relationship with Him. Do you see how that works? Often, we focus on the results we want and the changes we think we need to make without examining our hearts. We skip over the key step: examining our confidence in God to lead us to the result.

Last year, I had an opportunity to invest in professional training that would help me serve my clients on a deeper level. It wasn't cheap; honestly, the price tag made me hesitate more than once. I had bills and responsibilities, and this investment was not guaranteed to pay off. I could've easily played it safe, told myself, "Maybe later," as I've always done, or brushed it off as an investment I couldn't afford.

But something kept nudging me forward. I felt God's leading as if He were whispering, "I've called you to this; trust me with the details." After praying, crunching numbers with my husband, and honestly wrestling with my doubts, I decided to go for it. I signed up for the training, praying that God would provide and show me how to steward this decision well.

It hasn't been an overnight return; I am learning to market my services, be patient, and trust that God is moving behind the scenes. New clients are appearing, some referred by people I'd never met personally, others through unexpected networking opportunities. To my amazement, within a few months, the additional income will not only cover the cost of my training but exceed what I'd initially spent.

This experience has taught me a powerful lesson: walking in financial confidence doesn't mean having all the answers or money upfront. It means believing that if God's leading you to step out, He will also meet you there. By placing my faith in Him rather than my limited perspective, I discovered His provision could show up in ways I never saw coming. Since then, I'm approaching financial decisions with greater peace, knowing that my confidence isn't in the size of my bank account but in the faithfulness of the God who guides me.

So today, let's flip the script. Start by deepening your trust in Him. Let that trust and his record fuel your confidence in yourself and let that confidence guide the decisions that align with His word and purpose. That's where real transformation begins. God calls us to live confidently, not in our strength, but in His provision and promises. Financial confidence comes from trusting in God as our Source, believing He equips us with wisdom, courage, and the resources needed to steward our finances well. Today, we pray for boldness to walk it out; to step into financial decisions with faith and assurance.

Prayer

Faithful Father,

Thank you for being my firm foundation. You are my Provider, Sustainer, and the One who orders my steps. Because of you, I can walk boldly and confidently in every area of my life, including my finances.

Lord, I admit that there have been times when I lacked confidence, second-guessing myself, or hesitating to act because of fear or uncertainty. Today, I choose to place my complete trust in you. Your word reminds me in Proverbs 3:5-6 to trust in you with all my heart and lean not on my understanding. In all my ways, I acknowledge you, and you will direct my path.

Father, I pray for wisdom and discernment as I manage the resources you entrusted me. Just as Solomon prayed for wisdom to govern your people, I ask for wisdom to make sound financial decisions that honor you. I reject the spirit of confusion and doubt, declaring that you have given me a spirit of power, love, and a sound mind.

Lord, I believe that confidence in you is the key to financial freedom. I will not be shaken by economic uncertainty or the opinions of others. When the enemy tries to come in and destroy my confidence and discredit your work, help me to stand on your word. I will stand firm in the promises of your word, knowing that you are my source and supply. 1 John 5:14 tells us that this is the confidence that we have in you, that if we ask anything according to your will, you heareth me.

Thank you, Father, for equipping me to walk in financial confidence. I trust that you are guiding my steps, opening doors of opportunity, and providing everything I need to fulfill the purpose you have placed on my life. In Jesus' name, Amen.

Meditation Scriptures

- Philippians 1:6
- Hebrews 10:35-36
- 2 Corinthians 3:5

Reflection Questions

1. What does financial confidence look like in your life?

2. How can you rely on God's wisdom and guidance in your financial decisions?

____

____

____

____

____

____

____

3. How does trusting in God as your Source impact your confidence?

____

____

____

____

____

____

____

____

____

Notes

DAY 10

STAYING THE COURSE

"And let us not be weary in well doing: for in due season we shall reap, if we faint not." ~ Galatians 6:9

Financial breakthrough requires not only faith and vision but also perseverance. Even when the results we're hoping for remain unseen, God calls us to remain steadfast, consistently applying His principles and trusting that our sowing will yield fruit at the proper time. Today, we focus on staying consistent and faithful in our financial habits, confident that our labor in the Lord is never in vain.

When my husband and I prepared for our wedding, we committed to not being left with any debt once the day ended. We both agreed to consistently save $1,000 per month, knowing that we'd have about $24,000 in just over a year to cover our big day. We also understood that my parents couldn't cover those costs, so it was up to us to make it happen. Shameless plug, to hear more about my story, grab a copy of my book *"I Am Too Blessed to Be Broke: Breaking the Curse of Poverty Mindset in the Church"*. It was ambitious and a little intimidating for two "single" individuals preparing to merge their lives into one. But we were determined to stick to the plan.

Let me tell you, consistency was not easy. Saving that kind of money meant sacrifices that sometimes felt harder than they should have. We were two people from different financial habits, trying to prepare for a wedding and an entire life together. I had the vision and dream of the perfect wedding, the kind every girl dreams about. I'd catch myself wanting to spend extra here or splurge a little there to bring those dreams to life. Staying focused was tough, especially when the excitement of planning collided with the reality of sticking to a strict budget and goal.

And if that wasn't enough, we decided just four months before the wedding to purchase a house instead of renting an apartment. Talk about adding another layer of complexity! Now, we weren't just saving for a wedding but also preparing for one of our most significant financial decisions. Every dollar mattered, and every choice had to align with our priorities. It wasn't easy, but we knew our sacrifices would be worth it.

But giving up? That wasn't an option. We reminded ourselves that staying consistent wasn't just about the wedding day but the foundation we were building for our marriage. Every month, we stayed disciplined, making those deposits no matter how tempting it was to cut corners. And when the big day finally came, we enjoyed it fully, knowing we had paid for it all without a single penny of debt hanging over our heads.

That season taught us so much about commitment, discipline, and teamwork. Let me tell you, consistency isn't glamorous, it rarely is, but it's powerful. Our small, steady efforts created something beautiful and laid the foundation for how we'd approach finances as a couple moving forward. Staying the course wasn't just about pulling off a wedding but building a life together; one rooted in faith, discipline, and a shared vision for the future.

We couldn't see the complete picture then, but now, 13 years later, we're witnessing the fruit of those decisions. Remaining debt-free for our wedding and choosing to purchase a home before the big day laid the groundwork for the life we're living today. That home is now an investment property and brings in extra income monthly. While those choices weren't easy, they set us on a path of financial freedom and stability that we're still walking in.

And let me be honest, it was nothing but a God thing that two individuals in their early 20s remained consistent in paying tithes every month during that season. We didn't just tithe; we gave off our gross income; before taxes and benefits. Looking back now, I can see how significant that was. Even today, our tithes and offerings are non-negotiable. Being slightly transparent here, when I look at our budget, our tithes resemble a third mortgage payment every single month. Talk about the temptation to use that money for something else! But from the very beginning, we prayed that we would never waver in our position to give. And by God's grace, we haven't missed a paycheck or knowingly skipped an opportunity to honor Him with our finances.

That season wasn't just about meeting goals; it was about building habits and making decisions aligned with our faith and trust in God. Many people sought our help, but it would behoove us to remind them that consistency in giving and worship to God was the only way to explain our position. Even more incredible, this way of living wasn't just available to us; they had the same access and ability we had. Those lessons on consistency continue to guide us today, and they're a constant reminder of God's faithfulness when we ask Him to grant us the strength to stay consistent and steadfast.

Consistency is the bridge between where you are now, and the promises God has for your future. It won't always be easy, but staying disciplined and committed to your worship, giving, confidence, and positive mindset will yield results that exceed your expectations. Like me, you will face moments when giving up feels like an option, but it's not. Keep showing up, keep trusting, and keep moving forward. God honors consistency, and as you remain faithful, He will remain faithful to complete the good work He's started in you. Stay the course!

Prayer

God of Steadfastness,

I praise you for being the unchanging rock in a constantly shifting world. Your word encourages me in 1 Corinthians 15:58 to stand firm, let nothing move me, and always give myself entirely to your work, knowing that my labor in you is never wasted. Yet, I confess that there have been moments when discouragement has crept in—times when I've grown weary, doubted my efforts, or wondered if my consistent faithfulness would ever pay off.

Lord, today I ask you to fortify my spirit with steadfastness. Help me persevere in the assignments you've laid on my heart; wise budgeting, faithful giving, diligent saving, and honest stewardship. As Galatians 6:9 promises, when the breakthroughs I seek feel delayed, remind me that I am sowing seeds that will yield a harvest in due season if I do not give up.

Teach me, Father, to find joy in the process, not just the outcome. Renew my strength to continue doing what is right, trusting that you see every sacrifice, every wise decision, and every act of obedience. Let my consistency in financial matters testify to my trust in your provision, reflecting a faith that does not waver when results aren't immediate.

I surrender my impatience and frustration to you. Replace them with a patient endurance that mirrors the resilience of those in Scripture who labored faithfully and eventually witnessed your faithfulness. Align my heart so that I work not to earn your love or approval, both of which I already have, but to walk out the purpose you've given me in stewarding the resources entrusted to my care.

Thank you for empowering me to keep going, to remain steadfast, and to trust that my efforts, guided by your wisdom, will lead to the blessings you have for me. I will stay the course and count the cost. In Jesus' name, Amen.

Meditation Scriptures

- Galatians 6:9
- 1 Corinthians 15:58
- Hebrews 12:1

Reflection Questions

1. What practical steps can you take to maintain consistency in your financial habits?

____

____

____

____

____

____

____

____

2. How does seeing your financial actions as seeds sown for future harvest change your perspective?

Notes

DAY 11

BREAKING CHAINS, BUILDING LEGACY

"No weapon formed against you shall prosper, and every tongue which rises against you in judgment you shall condemn. This is the heritage of the servants of the LORD, and their righteousness is from me," Says the LORD.

~ Isaiah 54:17

Generational curses or behavior patterns, mindsets, and circumstances that seem to repeat from generation to generation can feel overwhelming. Whether it's financial struggles, poverty mindset, debt cycles, or limiting beliefs about money, these curses are often rooted in what we've seen, heard, or experienced growing up. They whisper lies like, "This is just how things are," or "This is all you'll ever know." But let me tell you, that's straight from the enemy.

These curses can hold us back financially, emotionally, and spiritually. They shift our focus from God's unmeasurable power to our finite and limited understanding. We lean on our strength, which only reinforces these unhealthy cycles. Breaking these curses isn't just about changing habits; it's about rejecting the narrative that has kept your family bound and replacing it with God's truth. It means acknowledging the cycles you've seen such as lack, fear, mismanagement, or an unwillingness to dream and choosing to rewrite the story. The struggles your family endured don't have to be your struggles. The mistakes of the past don't have to define your future.

As Christians, we know that when we accepted Christ, the curse was already broken through the covenant. But breaking free in the natural requires us to examine those patterns, pray through them, and take intentional steps toward freedom. I've had my own generational curses to break, though I'll keep the specifics to myself for now (my family hasn't signed off on me airing all the dirty laundry). Fear of success has been significant for me, and I've had to pray through it and take action to overcome it.

Here are a few generational cycles I've seen in our community:

1. **Lack of Financial Discussions -** Many of us weren't taught how to manage money growing up. Conversations about saving, credit scores, and budgeting didn't happen often. When kids asked questions about money, they were told to stay out of grown folks' business. Now, as an adult, we can see that it wasn't just about keeping secrets. Most households didn't have the knowledge or confidence to teach financial literacy.

2. **Low Priority on Paying Bills -** Have you ever heard the phrase, "They'll get their money when they get it"? Many households functioned this way, paying just enough to get by, and late fees always occurred. There was little urgency to

satisfy financial commitments, and frustration was often directed towards creditors rather than the poor habits or circumstances that led to an inability to meet the financial obligation.

3. **Belief That Winning the Lotto Is the Only Way to Wealth -** Some people genuinely believe winning the lottery is their only shot at financial freedom. Forget about working a fulfilling job, building a business, or investing; they've been conditioned to think large sums of money can only come through luck.

4. **Separating Health from Wealth -** There's often little emphasis on the connection between health and wealth. Taking care of your body (mentally and physically), eating right, exercising, and prioritizing wellness are often overlooked, even though these habits directly impact your ability to earn and enjoy wealth.

5. **"I'll Figure It out Later" Mentality -** Saving, contributing to a 401(k), getting insurance, or preparing for retirement is often seen as unnecessary or inaccessible. Some people think, "YOLO—enjoy life now and worry about the future later," while others assume they won't live long enough to retire. This mindset leaves many unprepared for life's later stages.

These are just a few examples. And let's not forget the fear of dreaming big, singing about a Big God every Sunday but not wholeheartedly believing He'll do big things for you. But breaking these curses isn't just about you; it's about the legacy you're building for your children or future generations. It takes prayer, intentionality, and faith. It means confronting the lies you've believed about money, standing firm in God's promises, and taking bold actions to rewrite the story.

Here's the good news: you don't have to do it alone. Galatians 3:13 reminds us that Christ has already redeemed us from the curse. Through Him, you can end generational poverty, fear, and lack. You can claim abundance, freedom, and wisdom; not just for yourself but for your family and future generations.

Today, let's identify patterns and cycles that no longer serve us and hand them over to God. Through prayer and intentional decisions, we can step into the freedom He's called us to. It's time to build a new foundation of faith, backed by prayer, and lasting change. Today, we draw a line in the sand and declare, "It stops with me."

Prayer

Almighty God,

I come before you today, boldly declaring that every generational curse in my life is broken in Jesus' name. Your word reminds me in Galatians 3:13 that Christ redeemed us from the curse of the law by becoming a curse for us. Through His sacrifice, I am set free from every chain of poverty, lack, and financial struggle that has held my family captive.

Lord, I renounce every negative pattern, mindset, or behavior passed down to me. I speak life and prosperity over myself and my family, declaring that financial hardship and mismanagement cycles end with me. As you promise in 2 Corinthians 5:17, I am a new creation in Christ. The old has gone, and the new has come. I claim this truth for myself and my descendants.

Father, I ask for your wisdom to identify areas where I may unconsciously perpetuate these curses. Reveal the habits, attitudes, or beliefs that do not align with your word. Give me the courage and strength to change them, leaning on your Spirit for guidance.

I thank you, Lord, for the blessings you have in store for my family. Deuteronomy 28:12 promises that you will open the heavens, the storehouse of your bounty, to bless all the work of our hands. I claim this promise for myself and declare that I will be the lender, not the borrower. My family's story will be one of abundance, generosity, and faithfulness to you.

In Jesus' name, I declare victory over every curse. My legacy will be one of freedom, prosperity, and unwavering trust in you. Amen.

Meditation Scriptures

- Galatians 3:13
- Exodus 20:6
- Isaiah 61:1
- Proverbs 13:22

Reflection Questions

1. Have you observed any negative financial patterns in your family and want to change them?

2. How can you break free from these patterns and create a new legacy?

3. What declarations can you speak over your finances and future generations today?

Notes

DAY 12

WALKING IN YOUR POWER, AUTHORITY, AND DOMINION

"Behold, I have given you authority to tread on serpents and scorpions, and over all the power of the enemy, and nothing shall hurt you." ~ Luke 10:19

Power, authority, and dominion are better known as our God-given superpowers. Yet, if we're honest, most Christians don't fully tap into them. We walk through life feeling defeated, overwhelmed, or unsure of our ability to stand firm, even though God has already equipped us with everything we need to overcome our challenges. Many Christians don't fully embrace these gifts, especially in our finances, often living as though we lack the strength, ownership, or right to make impactful decisions in our lives.

But let me remind you: when you are in Christ, you have dominion, which means ownership. You have authority, the right to act and make decisions, and the power and strength through Christ to enforce those decisions. Luke 10:19 reminds us that Christ has given us authority over the enemy and all his schemes. We weren't created to live timid, powerless lives. We are called to live boldly, exercising the dominion and authority given to us.

Now let's be honest: how often do we live like we own this power? Too frequently, we shrink back, unsure if we can handle what's in front of us. The truth is, we can't in our own strength, but through Christ, we have all the authority we need to claim victory. It's not about being perfect or having all the answers; it's about standing firm in faith, declaring God's promises, and using the power He's already given us.

As a part of the kingdom and body of Christ, He sat you above every wicked thing on this earth and has given you immeasurable power over everything through the Holy Spirit. The enemy can't invent anything that Christ doesn't have dominion over. Read that again if you must; let that marinate.

I'll be remiss if I don't say this. Too often, we hear teachings that make authority sound like a shortcut; *just declare it, and it's yours.* While our words absolutely carry weight in the spiritual realm, authority is not a magic trick, and dominion isn't passive. Relationship must be partnered with movement. God honors the believer who speaks the Word but also walks it out, even when it's hard. Your declarations don't just move the enemy; he's moved by your discipline, your obedience, and your unwavering trust in God's will, even when it doesn't look like victory yet.

Operating in dominion, authority, and power doesn't exempt us from process, pain, or pruning. It means we stand firm in who God says we are *through* the suffering, not just around it. This power isn't a "name it and claim it" lifestyle. It's a walk of bold faith and intentional stewardship. It's budgeting when you'd rather swipe. It's saving when you're believing for overflow. It's praying when you're in pain and still showing up on purpose. Authority is the ability to speak Heaven's language on earth and then live in a way that honors what you've said. In a way that honors God.

So yes, speak life. Declare provision. Walk in authority. But don't neglect the part of you that must be developed in the waiting. God's power flows through those who not only declare the promise but also partner with Him to carry it out. Faith without works is still dead, but faith that speaks and moves? That's when Heaven responds.

Prayer

Lord,

Thank You for the authority, dominion, and power You've given me through Christ. Not just to speak promises but to live them with discipline, obedience, and wisdom. Forgive me for the times I've expected a breakthrough without movement or spoken faith without matching it with action. Today, I choose to walk in alignment with Your Word, knowing that faith requires my active participation and stewardship is an integral part of my worship.

Help me take ownership of my finances, not with fear, but with clarity and courage. Teach me to honor You not just in declarations but in the day-to-day decisions—the budgets, the boundaries, and the sacrifices.

Give me discernment for what to do with what I have and the strength to follow through even when it's not easy.

Remind me that I am not powerless. I have the strength, the right, and the ownership to live the life You've called me to. Thank You for trusting me with this responsibility and empowering me to fulfill it. I declare that I will no longer live in fear or confusion about money. Instead, I will walk confidently, knowing You have already given me everything I need to manage well. You are my provider, and I honor You by stewarding what You've placed in my hands. In Jesus' name, Amen.

Meditation Scriptures

- Genesis 1:26
- Ephesians 1:19-21
- 2 Corinthians 10:4-5

Reflection Questions

1. What areas of your life have you avoided taking ownership of? How can you step into dominion over time?

____

____

2. How does knowing you have the authority to make decisions and enforce them with God's power change how you approach challenges?

Notes

DAY 13

YOU HAVE PERMISSION: JUST ASK

"And if we know that He hears us, whatever we ask, we know that we have what we asked of Him." ~1 John 5:15

Hold tight, this one was hard for me, but it must be said. How often do we hold back from asking God for what we truly need or desire? It could be fear of rejection, feelings of unworthiness, or simply not believing He will answer. Matthew 7:7-8 tells us, "Ask, and it will be given to you; seek, and you will find; knock, and the door will be opened to you." It's a promise! God is ready to bless us with wisdom, provision, and opportunities, but we must make the first move and ask through prayer. And if no one has told you, asking for help is okay. More importantly, it's okay to ask your Heavenly Father for what you need; not just to live life but to support the kingdom and experience joy.

If you're anything like me, asking for help doesn't come naturally. My hesitation started in childhood. Again, if you've read my book, *I Am Too Blessed to Be Broke: Breaking the Curse of Poverty Mindset in the Church*, you know I came from humble beginnings. I didn't want to stress my parents unnecessarily, so I started working and saving early. That's where my "Independent Woman" phase began. I was determined to handle things independently because I didn't want to be a burden. Besides, I'd seen my family's struggles, even though they managed to shield me from most of them. So, I only asked for help when I had no other option.

I still recall two moments in college when I asked for financial help outside of my parents: both times $20 until payday. That independent mindset carried into adulthood, where I believed, "If I can't do it myself, it's not meant to be done." When I got married, it took a while for me to let my guard down, but now? My husband would probably tell you I ask for everything!

But here's the thing: one day, I realized I'd been carrying that same mentality into my relationship with God. Deep down I was saying "God, you've already done so much for me, how dare I ask for more?" Unless it was a dire need, I rarely asked. I whispered small requests here and there; things like health, traveling mercies, or protection, but I avoided asking Him for anything financial.

And then during prayer one day, God stopped me. I felt Him ask, "Why didn't you ask me for that promotion? Why didn't you ask me to cover that bill before you scrambled to make ends meet? How big am I to you? Do you think I'm limited in resources?" That moment stopped me in my tracks.

It reminded me of Solomon in 2 Chronicles 6. Solomon stood before God, dedicating the temple, and prayed an extensive prayer, asking God to hear the prayers of His people and to cover Israel. That was a bold ask. He had the confidence to ask because he knew the character of God through the promises made to his father, David. And God responded. In fact, in the very next chapter, God sent fire down from heaven, filling the temple with His glory.

That's why we must be careful not to judge how someone else talks to or petitions God. I'll be honest. I remembered months earlier singing, "So arise from Your rest and be blessed by our praise," and telling my husband, “I don't know about that one. It feels a little off to be talking to God like that." However, I later learned that those lyrics were inspired directly by Solomon's prayer. The lyrics reflect the moment when the glory of the Lord filled the temple. And here I was, being "holy," critiquing what was scripture. Meanwhile, Solomon's bold ask pulled the glory of God down from heaven.

What am I saying? Don't let somebody else's "churchy" or "holier-than-thou" mindset stop you from asking God boldly. It might sound wild to others, but God understands the heart behind your ask. Solomon wasn't just throwing words around; he was standing in covenant. Solomon had already experienced the faithfulness of God's promises, and he knew God would honor His word. When Solomon placed the Ark of the Covenant in the temple, it was a declaration: this is the permanent resting place of God's presence with His people. And from that place, he appealed to God to hear the prayers of Israel, no matter what situation they faced.

Your ask is the same. It's not grounded in arrogance, but in the confidence and recognition of God's greatness, holiness, and covenant faithfulness. Even Solomon acknowledged that no temple could contain the fullness of God, yet he still asked—and God still answered.

That's what we miss sometimes. We tiptoe around God as if He can't handle our big asks, our raw prayers, or our needs. But scripture shows us otherwise. Repeatedly, God invites us to bring our requests and Jesus himself said in John 14:13–14, "And I will do whatever you ask in my name, so that the Father may be glorified in the Son. You may ask me for anything in my name, and I will do it." One of my favorite songs, written by the late Reverend Milton Brunson echoes this truth:

I'll give you peace when the storm is raging,
I'll be your light when the road ahead seems dim.
I have the power, just put your trust in Me.
Anything you need, have faith indeed.
Just ask, just ask, in My name.

I am the Lord, I can move all mountains,
I'll be your strength, when you're weary, weak and torn.
Believe in my promise. I will take care of you.
Anything you need, have faith indeed.
Just ask, just ask, in My name.

So where did this start? Many of us have been taught, either directly or indirectly, that going to God about wealth and money is blasphemous. That somehow asking Him for financial provision is selfish or unspiritual. God cares about every area of our lives, including our finances. His word says He wants us to prosper and live abundantly (3 John 1:2). Asking Him for financial wisdom, provision, and blessing is not only okay, but also what He desires. He's the ultimate provider, and when we ask, we're showing Him that we trust Him to lead us in every area, including our money.

As I deepened my relationship with God, I realized that my hesitation to ask wasn't always about "tradition" but faith. My ask was tied to my seek, and my seek was rooted in a lack of faith. It reminds me of being a child, wanting something but being afraid to ask because it felt too big. You don't want to get your hopes up or fear hearing "no." I'd brought God down to the level of man. I could believe Him to heal my body, protect my kids, or get me home safely, but not to do miraculous things in my finances.

When we don't ask, it limits what we allow God to do in our lives. He already knows what we need, but there's power in asking. It's an act of trust, faith, discipline, and obedience. When we ask, we show Him that we rely on Him, not ourselves. And the best part is you don't have to feel bad about what you have and receive because everyone can ask God for what they need. So today, let's break free from hesitation and boldly go before Him, trusting that He hears and answers.

God isn't intimidated by your ask. He isn't dismissing your cry. And He isn't limited in resources. But here's the balance we must hold; while the Word reminds us to ask, we must also remember who we're asking. God is not a genie we summon with perfect words or sacrificial giving in hopes of guaranteed outcomes. He is a sovereign King who is holy, wise, and deeply invested in our growth. Yes, He blesses, but He also leads, corrects, delays, and even says no when it's for our good.

Asking is our act of faith. Surrender is our act of trust. And trust is what keeps us connected when the answer doesn't come how or when we expected.

Prayer

God of Favor,

I come before you today with an open heart, ready to ask for what I need, knowing that you are a God who loves to give good gifts to your children. Lord, forgive me for the times I've held back from asking, whether out of fear, pride, or feelings of unworthiness. Remind me that you are not limited by the world's standards or by my circumstances.

Father, I admit I've found it easier to come to you about health, protection, or guidance, but I've hesitated regarding my finances. Forgive me for believing the lie that asking you for financial provision is wrong. You are the source of all things, including wealth, and your word says that you provide for your children abundantly. Today, I ask for wisdom to handle the resources you have given me, clarity in my financial decisions, and the courage to trust you with everything.

Just as Solomon stood before you and prayed that whenever your people turned toward your temple, you would hear them from heaven and answer, I ask the same today. Lord, when I lift my prayers about debt, about bills, about provision, about future goals, hear me from heaven. When I face lack, when I am tempted to fear, when I struggle to trust, hear me from heaven and move on my behalf. Let your presence fill my life the way your glory filled the temple, reminding me that you are near and attentive to my cry.

Help me to align my financial goals with your will. Give me a heart of stewardship and the boldness to seek your guidance in every area of my life, including my money. I thank you in advance for the answers you will provide, knowing that your plans are always for my good and your glory. In Jesus' name, Amen.

Meditation Scriptures

- Matthew 7:7-8
- James 4:2
- John 14:13-14
- 1 John 5:14

Reflection Questions

1. What is one financial decision ask you can take to God in prayer today?

Notes

DAY 14

BE A BLESSING, NOT JUST BLESSED

"You will be enriched in every way so that you can be generous on every occasion, and through us your generosity will result in thanksgiving to God."
~ 2 Corinthians 9:11

When we think about financial freedom, it's easy to focus on its benefits: less stress, more stability, and the ability to afford the life we've envisioned. But the truth is, God's plan for our financial lives doesn't stop with us. He blesses us so that we can, in turn, bless others, to be conduits of blessing, allowing God's provision to flow through us and impact the world around us.

A conduit is simply a channel, a vessel that connects one source to another. As believers, God calls us to be that channel, passing on His blessings to meet the needs of others, support His kingdom, and spread His love. This doesn't mean you have to be rich to bless others. It's not about the size of the gift but the heart behind it (I think you've heard that before). Whether you are tithing faithfully and cheerfully giving, or simply helping someone in need, every act of giving is an act of worship.

But let's be honest, being a conduit isn't always easy. It requires intentionality, trust, obedience, and sometimes sacrifice. You may be tempted to cling to what you've been given, fearing there won't be enough left. But here's the beauty of God's math: the more you give, the more He provides. 2 Corinthians 9:6-8 reminds us that God loves a cheerful giver and that when we give generously, He will ensure we have everything we need and even more to keep sharing.

Being a conduit of blessing also challenges us to think beyond ourselves. It's about shifting our perspective from "What can I get?" to "What can I give?" It's about realizing that your resources, money, time, and talents are tools God uses to fulfill His mission. When you step into this role, you bless others and experience the peace that comes from walking in obedience to God's voice.

Over the years, I've truly understood what it means to be a conduit. Should I say that God placed me in situations where I had no choice but to learn (those are never easy places)? For so long, I operated with a scarcity mindset. The thought of giving away what I wasn't sure would return or feeling like I needed to make up for lost time and missed opportunities was terrifying. I often thought, how can I help others when I'm barely helping myself?

But here's the thing about God: He knows exactly what and when you need it. And, of course, I married a husband who only knew how to give. He grew up in a home where generosity was a way of life. Don't get me wrong, I did as well and can't count the number of people I saw my parents help or those who lived with us, but as a preacher's kid, he'd seen firsthand the act of giving expanded across congregations. Let's say it was more natural for him to do.

One of my earliest lessons in giving came from something as simple as tipping at a restaurant. I'm ashamed to say this, but I was the type who wanted to leave the bare minimum, you know, 9.99%, and let's say my husband and I had more than a few "discussions" about what an appropriate tip should be. And by the way, I feel your judgment; this was twelve years ago when the standard was 10%. But through prayer, I began to see things differently. That's when I learned a simple yet profound formula: Giving + Giving = More for You to Give and Live. Again, the more you give, the more room you create for God to operate with His "God math" and multiply what you have.

I can't explain how God turned $5 into $5,203. But that's not for me to understand. It's about trusting Him. One of my mentors once said something that hit me hard: **"Some of us are too selfish to be wealthy."** Many of us don't have clarity on our wealth assignment nor understand that money is a tool and resource for doing what God has called us to do. Needless to say, this statement will permanently follow me through life.

It's not about giving to get; it's about being a vessel through which God's blessings flow. The more we release, the more He can trust us. Generosity isn't just a financial principle; it's a spiritual one.

And when we embrace it, we step into a life of abundance and purpose far beyond what we could imagine.

However, let's clarify something: a conduit of blessing doesn't mean you neglect your needs and wants or throw financial responsibility out the window. People often prey on givers, knowing they have a heart to give and, as the saying goes, would give the shirt off their back. But being a conduit of blessing is about more than just giving freely; it's about managing your finances to honor God while making room for generosity. It's about budgeting with intention, setting aside resources to give, and trusting that as you prioritize His kingdom, God will always provide for you.

Let's explain it this way: while God didn't bless me only to eat steak and lobster every day, He also didn't bless me to feel guilty about enjoying a fine dining experience. He blessed me to share that steak and lobster with my neighbor as often as He instructs me. It doesn't mean I can't have nice things and enjoy life; it means those blessings aren't meant solely for my selfish consumption.

I recently came across an article that argued Christians shouldn't buy luxury items or spend significant amounts of money on themselves, as we should be giving to those in need. Listen, I respect their perspective, but as for me and my house, there is a thing called balance. While I might have a luxury item or two, or even five, you'll never hear me say that I didn't pay my tithes and offerings. You'll never hear that I didn't volunteer or give back my time, that I ignored God's prompting to bless someone financially, or that I live extravagantly without acknowledging the needs of others.

The point is that God doesn't call us to extremes but to obedience and balance. His plan has room for both provision and generosity. Enjoy what He's blessed you with but always remember that those blessings come with a responsibility to share. It's not about what's in your closet or on your plate but what's in your heart.

So today, I challenge you to open your heart and hands. Ask God to show you how He wants to use you to bless others. It might look like giving to your church, supporting a friend in need, or sowing into a ministry close to your heart. Whatever it is, trust that your generosity will make an impact and bring glory to God. Remember, it's not about proving to your family, pastor, friends, or society what you can or cannot do; God is the only one who sincerely knows your heart. God's math is different, and He will multiply your seed if you trust Him.

Prayer

God of Provision,

Thank you for the resources you've entrusted to me. I recognize that everything I have comes from you, and I want to honor you by being a faithful steward of those blessings. Forgive me for the times I've held on too tightly to what you've given, forgetting that you are my ultimate provider.

Today, I ask you to help me become a conduit of blessing. Please open my eyes to the opportunities around me to give, serve, and support others. Teach me to trust that as I pour out, you will pour back into me, ensuring I have everything I need and more to continue giving.

Lord, I surrender my finances to you. Align my heart with your will so that my generosity reflects your love and provision. Show me where I can make a difference and remind me that every act of giving, no matter how small, is significant in your eyes. Thank you for the joy that comes from being a blessing to others. In Jesus' name, Amen.

Meditation Scriptures

- 2 Corinthians 9:6-7
- Proverbs 11:25
- Acts 20:35
- Luke 6:38

Reflection Questions

1. How do you view generosity? Is it something you prioritize, or does it feel like an afterthought?

2. What fears or hesitations do you have about giving? How can you surrender those to God?

Notes

STAY CONNECTED

PLUG IN TO PROTECT WHAT YOU'VE BUILT

"Do not be anxious about anything, but in everything by prayer and supplication with thanksgiving let your requests be made known to God. And the peace of God, which surpasses all understanding, will guard your hearts and your minds in Christ Jesus." ~Philippians 4:6-7

You've made it to the end! Money may be a resource, but what shapes how you use it is your heart. What's in your heart guides your actions. If selfishness or pride are rooted there, those will show up in how you spend, manage, and give. But if love, generosity, and integrity are there, those are the fruits that flow out.

That's why it's so important to guard your heart. Guarding your heart doesn't mean putting up walls; it means creating boundaries that protect your faith, your relationship with God, and the vision He's given you for your finances. When God's Word is the law, no distraction, fear, or circumstance can easily pull you off course.

But here's the key: guarding your heart and protecting what you've built requires more than good intentions. You must stay connected to the Source. As my pastor, James Perkins, Sr., said, "If something is going to sustain, last, or uphold, it has to be connected to a source." Think about it: a lamp can't shine without being plugged in, and your phone won't hold a charge if it never connects to power. In the same way, your spiritual and financial growth will not sustain unless you stay plugged into God through prayer, His Word, and obedience.

God is in the business of making sure you have what you need to be successful. The enemy has no power to bring you down from the level God desires you to live on. If you follow God's Word, He will bless and prosper you, and the devil can't stop Him. That's why prayer isn't optional; it's the lifeline that keeps your heart aligned, your mind clear, and your decisions unshakable.

If the results you've found in these last fourteen days have been helpful, what are you connected to that will help you sustain them? What practices, boundaries, and discipline will you carry forward to protect what God has started? Don't lose focus now. Stay connected, stay prayerful, and stay committed, because the seeds you've planted in these pages need watering to grow into the harvest God has promised.

This journey has been about so much more than budgets, numbers, and goals. It has been about realigning your heart with God's heart. If you want lasting change, you must stay connected to Him. Protect what you've built, guard your heart, allow him to be the source of your confidence, and keep drawing from the one who sustains it all.

As we close this chapter, I hope that every example, prayer, and scripture has stirred your faith and deepened your time with God. Don't stop here. Revisit this devotional whenever you need a reset or a reminder of God's instructions for you. Keep moving forward, trusting Him, and never lose focus. Greater is ahead.

Closing Prayer

Heavenly Father,

Thank You for every word, every scripture, and every moment spent with You through these pages. As I close this book, I don't close the journey. Keep my heart guarded, my mind focused, and my life connected to You; the true Source of everything I need. Teach me to walk in faith, to steward well, and to trust Your plan in every season. May my finances, my decisions, and my future always reflect Your goodness and glory. In Jesus' name, Amen.

ABOUT THE AUTHOR

Shavonna Perkins holds a degree in Accounting and multiple certifications in financial education and coaching. As the founder of The Confident Money Collective and The Bougie Wealth Group, she is dedicated to helping women transform their mindset, master their money, and maximize the luxury of financial freedom. Her expertise as a Certified Financial Education Instructor, along with years of professional experience in the financial services industry, has positioned her as a trusted voice in both faith and finance.

Growing up in poverty in one of the poorest counties in North Carolina, Shavonna experienced firsthand the weight of financial lack and a struggle with self-confidence. Yet, through faith, discipline, and perseverance, she turned her story of scarcity into one of confidence and freedom. Her journey has ignited a passion to empower others to break generational cycles, walk boldly in their God-given authority, and embrace financial clarity as a form of freedom.

Today, Shavonna serves as The Confident Money Coach, an author, speaker, and mentor using her testimony to inspire women to trust God in every season of life. With a unique blend of biblical wisdom and practical financial strategies, she equips her community not only to manage money but also to cultivate confidence, purpose, and peace.

LET'S STAY CONNECTED

1 **LEAVE A REVIEW** – Your feedback matters! A quick review on Amazon helps other readers who need this message discover it too.

2 **JOIN MY EMAIL LIST** – Be the first to know about new resources, upcoming events, and special opportunities. Visit www.shavonnaperkins.com to sign up today.

3 **INVITE ME TO SHARE** – If you'd like to introduce this devotional to your group, host a workshop, or invite me as a speaker, I'd be honored to connect. Reach out through my website to explore how we can make it happen.

www.ingramcontent.com/pod-product-compliance
Lightning Source LLC
LaVergne TN
LVHW010926110826
845149LV00013B/2497

* 9 7 9 8 9 9 9 4 9 7 2 0 8 *